50 THINGS TO REALIZE BEFORE IT'S TOO LATE

MANOJ CHENTHAMARAKSHAN

Made with ♥ on the Notion Press Platform
www.notionpress.com

Contents

Contents

Contents

Acknowledgements

I'd like to express my gratitude to Sneha Murali for her unwavering support and patience throughout this journey as I pursued even my most unconventional ideas.

Introduction

In this book, I have chosen to break away from the traditional format of writing. Instead of trying to prove a point, my goal with this book is to make readers think for themselves.

Throughout my thirties, I have gone through many experiences and learned many valuable lessons. This book is simply an expression of all these learnings. I have included many different topics in this book, some of which may seem to contradict each other.

But that is the nature of life - things are not always black and white. What we believe to be true is often subject to change and evolution. I encourage you to read this book with an open mind, and consider the ideas and perspectives presented with a sense of curiosity and objectivity.

I must mention that none of the content in this book is original, it's the learnings that I have gained by studying and experiencing some great works left behind by some of the world's most influential figures.

"Everything that needs to be said has already been said. But since no one was listening, everything must be said again." - *Andre Gide*

CHAPTER ONE

WHY NOT LIVE NOW?

"Most humans are never fully present in the now, because unconsciously they believe that the next moment must be more important than this one. But then you miss your whole life, which is never not now. And that's a revelation for some people: to realize that your life is only ever now."
-Ekhart tolle

I have come across the idea of living in the present moment without worrying about the future or setting goals. At first, it seemed foolish to me as I had been taught throughout my life that everything should be done with a specific outcome in mind.

Doing something without considering the outcome or potential results seemed like a waste of time. As a result, I found myself constantly comparing my life to how I thought it should be, rather than focusing on what I needed to do to achieve my goals.

As I worked tirelessly towards my goals, I felt frustrated

and anxious. I would have occasional moments of happiness, but they were fleeting.

One day, I watched a video by Ankur Warikoo and he said, ***"Do what you love with no expectation and you will not only get a magnificent result but also enjoy each day."*** I didn't fully understand this concept at first, but after watching the video multiple times, it clicked for me.

We often have a destination in mind and work hard to reach it, but as we work towards it, we become hard on ourselves for not being there yet. This leads to an increasing sense of frustration as our vision of where we should be doesn't match our current reality.

I realized that I was not happy with my daily life and that my habitual mindset of always being busy and stressed had awakened me to this fact. I then started writing books without any specific outcome in mind, but simply because I enjoyed it.

This book was written without any expectation or agenda, it was completed simply because of the pleasure of expressing oneself.

Consider applying this mindset to your own life. Give it a try for a week and do what you love without any expectations. You will be amazed by the results. When you stop thinking about impressing others, you become less susceptible to peer pressure and more authentic.

Is it necessary to have an end goal? Yes, it is important to have a direction in mind, but don't become overly focused on the final outcome. Instead, find joy in the journey that takes you to your destination.

"When you're happy, it's as though the entire universe is conspiring on your behalf and presenting whatever you need in the moment you need it."
-RHONDA BYRNE From The Greatest Secret

CHAPTER TWO

BEING YOURSELF

"Existence wants you to be you."
- Osho

The easiest and most effortless way to excel at something is to simply be true to yourself.

Being yourself means being authentic and not hiding your true thoughts and feelings. No matter what your profession is, whether you're a graphic designer, architect, accountant, or doctor, you have unique perspectives and ideas that should be shared without hesitation.

As Mahatma Gandhi said, ***"Happiness is when what you think, what you say, and what you do are in harmony."*** Expressing yourself means doing what you truly want to do, rather than what you feel you should do. You may think, *"But I have responsibilities, what will others think?"* But ask yourself, how long are you willing to continue doing an injustice to yourself by not being true to who you are?

Participating in activities you enjoy and expressing your views doesn't require anyone's permission, only your own.

Even in difficult situations, leaders like Mahatma Gandhi and Nelson Mandela were true to themselves and expressed themselves authentically.

The only person stopping you from being yourself is yourself, the little voice in your head that says, *"I can't do it, I'm stuck in life."* But remember, there is also a quieter voice that says, *"Why not try? I'll be happy," or "I want to give it a try."*

Choose to increase the volume of the voice that supports you and decrease the one that holds you back. Understanding these two voices is a topic for another discussion, but for now, remember to be yourself. The world needs to see the unique and authentic version of you, just as nature needs the diversity of different trees, plants, and creatures in the forest.

Short story:
A French couple, an Irish couple, and a Polish couple are having dinner together. The Frenchman says to his wife, *"Pass me the sugar, Sugar."* Not to be outdone, the Irishman says, *"Could you pass me the honey, Honey?"* Most impressed by these clever endearments, the Pole leans over to his wife and says, *"Pass me the pork, Pig."* Avoid copying; otherwise, you will do something stupid.

CHAPTER THREE

SMILE

"Nothing kills the ego like playfulness, like laughter. When you start taking life as fun, the ego has to die, it cannot exist anymore." -Osho

Your life can change for the better when you smile, even during the toughest of times. When you smile, even the most difficult problems can seem insignificant. Despite the fact that this power is readily available to us, many of us do not fully appreciate it.

Smiling triggers the release of happy hormones in the brain, making it easier to handle any situation. A study was conducted with two groups of people who were asked to complete a difficult task. The first group was instructed to hold a pencil horizontally in their mouths while performing the task, and the second group was asked to complete the task without the pencil.

At the end of the experiment, the group who held the pencil reported that the task was enjoyable and exciting, while the group who did not hold the pencil found the task boring and complicated.

While it may seem like the pencil was the key factor, the real magic was in the facial expression. Try holding a pencil or pen horizontally in your mouth and biting down on it. The facial muscles you use are similar to those used when smiling, which triggers the release of happy hormones, making any task feel more enjoyable.

It's that simple, so next time you find yourself feeling bored or anxious about a task, try smiling while you do it. You'll be surprised by the difference it makes. And remember to pass this tip along to others throughout your day, you'll find many opportunities to smile.

Just smile, my friend, it's that easy.

"As soap is to the body, so laughter is to the soul."
- A Jewish Proverb

CHAPTER FOUR

WHO AM I TO JUDGE?

"Be so busy Improving your self that you have no time to criticize others."
- Chetan Bhagat

I was at the gym and overheard some of my fellow gym-goers gossiping about celebrities. They were speaking as if they knew the celebrities personally and had formed negative opinions about them based on a single news article they had read online.

I couldn't help but wonder if even the celebrities themselves had as much information about themselves. I also pondered why people engage in this behavior, why they feel the need to judge others.

After some research, I discovered that there are various reasons that might lead people to gossip. They may be envious of the person's life, have had negative experiences in childhood, or have grown up in a household where gossiping was a common occurrence.

People often gossip to feel a sense of security and to present a positive image to the outside world.

It doesn't matter if it's a celebrity or your neighbor, gossiping is pointless. While you're judging and criticizing others, the person you're talking about is likely taking action and moving forward.

There is a new trend of online trolling, which is just another form of bullying. I have personally unfollowed many online channels for this reason, as I found that their constant negativity was affecting my own individuality.

My advice is to avoid such channels or pages and instead focus on being original in your thoughts and judgments.

As I wrote this, I realized that I, too, may be guilty of judging others based on their behavior. However, I believe there is a difference between judging and observing, and I am trying to understand the patterns and psychology behind this behavior.

"When you judge others, you do not define them, you define yourself."
- Earl Nightingale

CHAPTER FIVE

WE DONT SEE THE SAME

"The meaning of communication is the result you get"
- Richard Bandler

Recently, my partner and I were discussing a video we had watched together. To my surprise, what she saw and understood from the video was vastly different from my own perception. When I shared my understanding with her, she mentioned that she hadn't noticed any of the things I had.

This got me thinking, how two individuals can watch the same video but perceive it so differently. We all have filters through which we interpret and understand information. We often assume that the receiver will understand exactly what we are saying, but in reality, they have their own filters that can modify and change the message.

The field of NLP (Neuro-Linguistic Programming) suggests that we use three filters while processing information: deletion, distortion, and generalization.

For example, in a conversation between Person A and Person B:
Person A: I am hungry, let's eat.
Person B: Let's go to a restaurant.
Person A: I don't want to eat at a restaurant.
Person B: Let's cook at home then.
Person A: Why do you do this every time? My parents' house is nearby, let's go there to eat.

In this scenario, Person A deleted the information that they wanted to go to their parents' house to eat, leading Person B to distort the message by suggesting eating at a restaurant. Person A then generalizes this problem by asking *"Why do you do this every time?"*.

This conversation could have been much simpler if Person A had clearly communicated their desire to go to their parent's house to eat. But often, when we spend a lot of time with someone, we expect them to be able to read our minds. This is not always the case.

It's important to keep in mind that when we communicate, we all have our own unique perspectives and filters that can affect how we interpret and understand information. This applies not only to the receiver of the message but also to the person communicating it.

When you are trying to express yourself and wondering why the other person isn't understanding you, try to communicate clearly and without any filters. It's unrealistic to expect someone to read between the lines and understand hidden meanings in your words. Instead, try to communicate as if you were meeting this person for the first time, and be patient in your communication.

"Maturity is when you accept that everyone has their own perspectives"

CHAPTER SIX

CHANGE IS A NATURAL PROCESS, EVOLUTION REQUIRES EFFORT

It is a common belief that people change over time, both physically, mentally and emotionally. However, true personal growth and evolution requires conscious effort and dedication. Similar to building muscle, it is not a natural process, but one that requires time and energy.

This also applies to our mental and emotional well-being, as it is important to be mindful of our choices in terms of food and the information we consume. Even two people of the same age can have vastly different physical, mental and emotional states, depending on the choices they have made in their lives.

I recently had the opportunity to meet with friends from college after a decade had passed. As expected, everyone had changed in their own unique ways. Some were married, some had children, and others had moved abroad. Those who had immediately taken on jobs after college had a different life experience than those who had not. Some had settled into a comfortable and safe lifestyle, even accumulating debt early on, just to fit in with their social circle. However, others had pursued their passions, even if it meant working late, and had a distinct lifestyle from the rest.

It can be challenging to stand out and commit to one's own unique path, especially when friends are financially stable. But it is important to remember that the person who takes the extra step of exploring themselves and their abilities, tend to live a more fulfilling life. Though, it is important to note that even those who choose to find themselves may have their own set of problems, but the way they handle them is different.

Change happens to everyone, but only a select few truly evolve. The individuals who evolve are those who do not seek comfort, but instead, strive to discover their true abilities. One can imagine, if fish had not attempted to walk on land millions of years ago, the humanity wouldn't be reading this right now.

"Change is inevitable, Growth is optional"
- John Maxwell

CHAPTER SEVEN

THE LITTLE VOICE OF DOUBT

As the night grew later, I found myself sitting in front of my computer, ready to post a candid video about my life. But just as I was about to hit the "**publish**" button, a small voice inside my head began to speak up. *"Who would notice if you missed a day?"* it whispered. *"Now is not the right time to post informational content,"* it said. *"Who wants to know about your life? It's not shareable content. Why don't you just share something like everyone else?"*

The voice almost convinced me not to post the video, but I shook my head and pressed the button anyway. To my surprise, within just a few minutes, the video had reached 4,500 people and had been shared more than 21 times. Someone even left a comment saying thank you for sharing my story.

This experience made me reflect on the voice inside my head that had almost held me back. It's a voice that we all have, and it can be a powerful force in our lives.

An old Cherokee chief once taught his grandson about this inner voice.

"A fight is going on inside me," the chief said.

"It's a terrible fight and it's between two wolves.

One is evil -- he is anger, envy, sorrow, regret, greed, arrogance, self-pity, guilt, resentment, inferiority, lies, false pride, superiority, self-doubt, and ego.

The other is good -- he is joy, peace, love, hope, serenity, humility, kindness, benevolence, empathy, generosity, truth, compassion, and faith.

The same fight is going on inside you and inside every other person, too."

The grandson asked, *"Which wolf will win?"*

The chief simply replied, *"The one you feed."*

We all have this inner voice and it's important to be aware of it. Sometimes, it can hold us back from expressing ourselves or achieving our goals. But by recognizing it and actively choosing to feed the positive voice, we can overcome it and make progress in our lives.

One way to do this is to identify the negative statements that we tell ourselves, and then create a new list of positive affirmations that counter those statements.

For example, if we tell ourselves *"I am shy, I am not*

confident enough to share my thoughts with the world," we can counter that with *"I am confident, I have the energy to share my thoughts with the world, I believe in myself."*

It's important to remember that this inner voice will continue to appear, but by practicing self-awareness and repeating these positive affirmations, we can overcome it and continue to evolve

"Have you realized that most of your unhappiness in life is due to the fact that you are listening to yourself instead of talking to yourself?"
- Martyn Lloyd Jones

CHAPTER EIGHT

HUMANITARIAN LEADERS

There is no doubt that in the current world, we are building more educated individuals with visions and the ability to think beyond. Children are trained at a young age to think about landing on the moon and making their nation proud, but it's important to consider whether this education is helping us sustain and survive as humanity for the next 100 years. The world doesn't need more intelligent people, but people with kindness in their hearts.

Unfortunately, in today's generation, educated minds are often using their knowledge to find loopholes and profit for themselves, rather than using it to serve and help others. Education without instilling humanity can lead to a future generation that is cynical and selfish.

"We have developed speed, but we have shut ourselves in. Machinery that gives abundance has left us in want. Our knowledge has made us cynical. Our cleverness, hard and unkind. We think too much and feel too little. More than machinery we need humanity. More than cleverness we need

kindness and gentleness. Without these qualities, life will be violent and all will be lost... The aeroplane and the radio have brought us closer together. The very nature of these inventions cries out for the goodness in men - cries out for universal brotherhood - for the unity of us all."
- Charlie Chaplin, The great dicator

It's important to find balance in education and instill values such as kindness and empathy, so that the future generation can coexist on this planet. Religions are many but still we unite in the name of humanity, Countries are many but still we unite in the name of humanity, Skin colors are many but still we unite in the name of humanity.

"We can live without religion and meditation, but we cannot survive without human affection."
- Dalai Lama

CHAPTER NINE

JUST FLOW

"Support your soul to express and experience things in this world, Never be the one who is blocking yourself"

My heart was pounding as I was the next speaker at an event in Mumbai. Despite having given speeches more than 50 times, I couldn't help but feel anxious as there were business gurus in the audience who had more experience and knowledge than myself. I even wished that the whole event would flop so I wouldn't have to give the speech.

Two weeks prior, I had been excited about the opportunity to speak, but everything turned upside down as the day arrived. I had all the symptoms of stage fright, even though I had given speeches many times before. This was different, however, as it had been two years since I had presented on stage due to COVID-19.

As I walked up to the stage, something unexpected happened. The host struggled to pronounce my second name, "Chenthamarakshan," and instead said "Chenthakrish" and "Chenmark." I simply giggled and corrected him. This simple act of laughing helped ease the tension, and I was no longer concerned about what people would say.

I spoke from my heart for the next 10 minutes and was in a flow state. Time seemed to stop for me as I spoke. During the 8th minute, I became aware that I was speaking and saw myself as if I was a spectator. The audience was attentive and kept their phones down to listen, and at the end, I heard claps from the crowd. People even came up to me personally to thank me. So, what happened there? What shifted my anxiety into a flow state?

Laughing helped ease the tension before going on stage and made me more comfortable in my own skin. When I stopped trying to impress people and make them like me, I began speaking from my heart. I let my soul take control of my body and let my intellectual and logical mind take a back seat for 10 minutes.

Deep down, we all know what would make our soul smile, but our ego often gets in the way. It wants to protect us, but in the process, it stops us from trying new things and being comfortable with who we are. It takes courage to let go of the ego and tap into our soul. Trust me, when you stop listening to the ego and tap into your soul, things start to flow.

We all have access to a universal energy within us that is available for free. Close your eyes, calm your mind, and listen to what your soul wants to express through this life form. Be the medium through which the universe can communicate.

"Flow is an optimal state of consciousness, a peak state where we both feel and perform our best. We become so involved in an activity that nothing else seems to matter. The ego falls away. Time flies. Every action, movement and thought follows inevitably from the previous one, like playing jazz. Your whole being is involved, and you're using your skills to the upmost."

- Mihaly Csikszentmihalyi

CHAPTER TEN

GOOD PEOPLE HAVE AN INFERIORITY COMPLEX

"Fear and self doubt have always been the greatest enemies of human potential"
- Brian Tracy

I am a big fan of speaker Suki Sivam and one of his speeches resonated with me particularly. He mentioned a quote that goes *"the problem in the current world we live in is that good people are feeling inferior, while those causing harm to the world are walking with complete confidence."*

I can relate to this statement as I am a positive individual who is determined to make a positive impact in the world and earn money through good deeds. I believe that positivity is the cure for many of the world's problems. But when it comes to selling my ideas or products, I tend to hold back and doubt myself.

I often think to myself, *"How can I sell?" "I don't know how to sell?" "People will recognize me for my work; why should I market myself?"*

On the other hand, those who sell harmful products such as energy drinks, are so confident in their marketing and have entire teams of high-paid employees to do so.

Why is this the case in the world? Shouldn't it be the opposite? Some companies do start with good intentions and make a positive impact on the world, but they are in the minority.

If you are reading this, I believe that you are a good person too. You need to stand up for your views, believe in yourself, trust your instincts and trust in other good people in this world. When you have confidence in yourself, you become an inspiration to others around you. This ripple effect slowly grows, and it becomes a massive wave. It takes time, but the change will begin with you.

Stand up for yourself, there's a child 20 years from now who will be grateful for you!

CHAPTER ELEVEN

HEALTH IS WEALTH

"Take care of your body. It's the only place you have to live."
- Jim Rohn

I had known this quote for a long time, I had seen it on Pinterest and heard it from my teachers, but I never paid much attention to it. However, it hit me hard when I fell sick in April 2022. I had a fever, cold, and headache that lasted for over ten days and left me feeling completely frustrated. I had to isolate myself to avoid spreading it to others.

During this time, I couldn't think straight, I wanted to write but couldn't form the words, and I wanted to speak but my throat hurt. I couldn't even do the things I loved to do. I was wondering, "*What the hell, dude?*"

I hated sleeping all the time and felt unproductive, but I couldn't work either. Can you understand what I'm trying to say here? You may have experienced something similar when you were ill.

This experience made me pause and reflect for a moment. Even if I had loads of money, even if I had a Rolls Royce parked in my garage, even if I had a two-way ticket to Las Vegas with my wife, if I had poor health, my bed would be my only companion. How hard is that?

Sometimes we have to learn things the hard way, and this time it hit me really hard. I am now realizing the importance of exercise and eating healthy. Let me tell you, our body is the medium through which we experience this world, and it should be our utmost priority to take care of it.

We are all going to experience death; it is an inevitable truth. No one has ever escaped it. As we age, we will experience discomfort, but as you are reading this, you do have the energy. Don't take it for granted. So, don't wait until you fall sick to realize the importance of taking care of your health. You can start taking care of it today.

"The man who earns a million, but destroys his health in the process is not really a success."
– Zig Ziglar

CHAPTER TWELVE

ATTRACT GOOD PEOPLE

"Things are never quite as scary when you've got a best friend."
- Bill Waterson

As I was isolated in a room (due to being sick), I was watching a series and resting. I received a call from a friend who I consider to be like a sister. We spoke for almost 50 minutes, and I was surprised by where the conversation started and where it led. There was no intention for the call, it was purely out of love.

She started to express concern for my health and my being single, even though I had turned 30. Although I had always been against the idea of marrying within a certain age, I listened to her patiently because her words came from a place of pure love and concern for me.

I felt relieved when the call ended. I realized that it's not about having intellectually or financially successful friends, but having kind and good-hearted friends who expect nothing but your presence.

I am not someone who maintains friendships, like how some people stay in touch for an extended period. I live in my own world without speaking with anyone for months, but when I do talk with someone, I give them my full attention which makes the conversation more meaningful.

When I reflect upon the people I have met and have a good rapport with, they all have one thing in common: they are good people. They are kind-hearted and expect nothing in return but support when in need.

If you have kind souls in your circle, keep them close. These people may not be wealthy or intellectually accomplished enough to help you in your career, they may not be physically close to you, but when there is a need, their emotional support will give you the strength you need.

Boy: *"What is important? The journey or the destination?"*
Wise man: *"The company"*

Cherish the kind-hearted people in your life, they will help you through the ups and downs of life.

CHAPTER THIRTEEN

FAITH RESTORED

To be honest, I didn't like living in India. I believed that other countries were far ahead in terms of human development and thought processes, and I thought living in India felt like traveling 20 years backward. I tried various ways to leave India, believing that it would solve the problem, but it was not the country itself that was the issue, it was the people running the country.

However, my perspective changed completely when I visited a school called "**NEXT School**" in Mumbai. As I entered the school, the first thing I saw was a group of young children learning yoga in an unconventional way. The teacher was making noises like an elephant and dog while leading the poses, and the children were having fun. I was struck by the contrast to my own school days where laughing was discouraged.

I also had the opportunity to meet the co-founder of the school, who I had initially misjudged as a student due to his casual appearance. But as he spoke, I began to understand his vision for the school.

They followed a system called "The Big Picture," which emphasized practical, real-world learning. The children were encouraged to explore their strengths and experiment with themselves.

We all have learned $(a+b)^2 = a^2 + b^2 + 2ab$. But to date, I haven't used this formula in my lifetime. I am sure that you haven't as well. But I was made to believe that if I didn't know this formula, I would be a failure in life. In this school, they have ensured that all the teachings should be useful in the real world. They have created a space for children to explore their strengths and experiment with themselves.

I realized that my thought process was the problem and not the country itself. The change-makers are few, and if leaders originated from schools like this, I believe the country would be prosperous. I am glad that in some parts of the world, there are passionate people who value others' perspectives and are working to restore the planet.

My faith gets restored when I see such passionate people.

CHAPTER FOURTEEN

SOME DAYS ARE SHIT

It's not possible to stay positive the entire life, and hey, that's ok!

CHAPTER FIFTEEN

RESOLVE PAST CONFLICTS

Not resolving the past conflicts is like carrying an explosive with you everywhere. Once you resolve it wholeheartedly, you will simply defuse it. If you don't, you will never know when the bomb will explode and it may hurt the ones close to you.

I was having a conversation with my partner when what started as a casual conversation became a huge fight. The entire day started to look bad. I didn't want to solve it until waking up the next day morning. Upon reflecting on the crux of the problem, I realized that it was not the conversation that originated the problem but an incident that happened a year back.

It rose up to the surface because I didn't resolve it. We spoke about it and gave each other's perspectives on the situation, but it was not solved. When we were speaking casually, this unresolved memory just flashed, and the argument started.

We often think we have a misunderstanding with another person because of a particular situation, but we should be also aware that we are memory machines. We carry memory everywhere we go in this lifetime. These memories can be pleasant or unpleasant. If we don't resolve the past memories where there was a conflict, it simply stacks up. You may not be aware of it, but these memories dictate into belief systems.

You start to build a mental picture about a person, start associating words, beliefs and values with the individual. This mental picture keeps evolving as you spend time with the individual. Until you come to peace with the unresolved memory, you keep feeding this mental picture with new information.

When you resolve a fight or a miscommunication with your partner, ensure to resolve it completely. If you leave it vaguely, chances are that it will rise back again. So what to do now?

The first step starts with you, Self-reflect with yourself to come to a conclusion, Respect the other person's viewpoint and forgive them. You may now say that *"Hey, why should I forgive when I didn't commit any mistake?"*. Well when you forgive them from your mind, you hold no grudge or negativity in your mind.

Remember that the negativity may or may not be in the other person, but when you hold a grudge or discomfort about another person, it exists in your mind and therefore it exists in you. You may justify that it's your perception, but it can't define your individuality, but unfortunately it does.

This simple concept of your memories affecting your well-being is understood by Hawaiians. They have created a healing technique called Ho'oponopono, where they use these four phrases to clean themselves spiritually:

"I am sorry, Please forgive me, Thank you, I love you!"

These statements are not to be said to anyone but ourselves. When we say ***"I am sorry,"*** we are taking 100% responsibility; ***"Please forgive me"*** allows you to let go of your ego; ***"Thank you"*** allows you to mentally accept that it's been resolved; and ***"I love you"*** allows you to find peace with the individual or situation.

Remember that this practice is not necessary to be verbally spoken to another person. It is to be practiced with yourself. Like a mantra, start repeating these in your mind. When you witness an unresolved memory rising into your awareness, repeat these phrases. You will start to feel the peace within you. If you need external help, visit a counselor who will help you overcome this situation.

"The purpose of life is to be restored back to Love, moment to moment. To fulfill this purpose, the individual must acknowledge that he is 100 percent responsible for creating his life the way it IS. He must come to see that it is his thoughts that create his life the way it is moment to moment.The problems are not people, places, and situations but rather the thoughts of them. He must come to appreciate that there is no such thing as "out there."

- Ihaleakala Hew Len

CHAPTER SIXTEEN

LIFE IS A GAME, PLAY IT

Life is often compared to a game, but why do we tend to become so serious at times? Is it because society tells us that maturity means keeping a straight face? Somewhere along the way, we've convinced ourselves that maturity means living a serious life.

I'm not sure how or why this happened, but many of us can admit that we've started taking life too seriously. We search for meaning in everything we come across, we want to know the exact path to take, and we become unhappy when faced with obstacles. I am no exception to this; just because I am discussing this topic, it doesn't mean that I haven't taken life seriously in the past.

However, I am beginning to realize that this way of living is not working. I want to live a joyful and fun-filled life, but it's almost impossible to do so when constantly analyzing everything.

Instead, I've decided to focus on doing things I love.

Whether I see immediate results or not doesn't matter, as long as I am happy every day. When we do this, we elevate ourselves; we don't need validation or recognition, we're like a child playing in the mud. This is when we start to live life passionately and do great work.

Sometimes we may stray from this way of thinking, but we can always remind ourselves that life is a game. There is no winning or losing, only enjoying the process.

I sometimes drift from this mindset, but reading and learning from online mentors helps me get back on track.

Why not try this for yourself? Stop planning every move and focus on being happy in the present moment, doing things that bring you joy. Allow ideas to come naturally.

When you approach life from this perspective, things become easier. Life becomes manageable. The greatest gift we've been given is the ability to think and act on our thoughts. Let's use it for our benefit, instead of worrying.

"Take Life Easily, Lovingly, Playfully, Non-seriously. Seriousness Is A Disease, The Greatest Disease Of The Soul And Playfulness The Greatest Health."
- OSHO

"I don't think existence wants you to be serious. I have not seen a serious bird. I have not seen a serious sunrise. I have not seen a serious starry night. It seems they are laughing in their own ways, dancing in their own ways. We may not understand it, but there is a subtle feeling that the whole existence is a celebration."

- *Osho*

CHAPTER SEVENTEEN

SW,SW,SW,SW

I heard this quote from a person I admire "Nithya Shanthi". I'm not sure if he quoted it, but he shared it with me.

"Some will, some won't, so what? Someone's waiting."

Read it again. How simple and profound, right? When I was stuck with the self-doubt of whether I should write books or not, whether people would accept me, and what if I'm wrong, I had many confusions, and then this beautiful quote came to me.

This is how I interpreted the quote:
Some people will want to read your books,
Some won't like your books,
So what if they don't like it?
Someone is waiting for your upcoming books.

When I realized that someone was waiting for my books, I stopped my self-doubt. All this time, I was worried about criticism, even though it was less than 5% of the entire audience. I was focusing too much energy on the naysayers. How self-absorbed and selfish of me to only think about my social image, instead of acknowledging the people who appreciate my work?

Can you relate to this in your life, my friend? Let your soul express what it wants to express. Your fear of rejection is tiny compared to the benefit it will do for someone else's life. Don't stop the potential of helping those who need you just because you want to protect your self-image.

I was once coaching a client who wanted to speak about women's empowerment. Being a victim of abusive relationships, she wanted to spread awareness about abusive behaviors and countermeasures to defend themselves. I was moved and touched by it, but apparently, she thought to herself, *"Who am I to tell this?" "I am not qualified enough."*

I told her, *"Because of your self-doubt, many women aren't aware of abusive behaviors. And as we are speaking right now, some women are facing these issues at this very moment. Don't let them suffer because of your self-doubt. Do what feels right and stop listening to the fear."*

I want to say the same to you. Some will, some won't, so what? Someone is waiting. Whatever your gift is, start sharing it with the world. It could be art, music, dance, accounting, engineering, robotics, poetry, teaching, or building a rocket to Venus. Go ahead and do it; someone is waiting for you.

"You yourself, as much as anybody in the entire universe, deserve your love and affection."
- Buddha

CHAPTER EIGHTEEN

STOP CONSUMING RANDOM SHIT

Yes, I am talking about social media. We are constantly feeding our minds with unwanted information. In the past, we used to observe older people gossiping and talking for hours on end. Now, we are doing the same thing on social media - it has just evolved in form.

I noticed myself endlessly scrolling through social media day after day, and at the end of the day, I felt like the day had just flown by. In reality, it hadn't flown by; I had just wasted my energy on things that brought no benefit to my life. This realization hit me hard when I stopped creating and started consuming. I would have an idea, but instead of acting on it, I would scroll through videos online and watch them. Slowly, my interest would disappear.

Victor Frankl, the author of the famous book "**Man's Search for Meaning,**" written in 1946, said, *"If we don't* *find meaning, we start to distract ourselves."* How true is that when applied to the modern world? In our modern world, boredom is very rare in our lives because we always have a distraction machine that we carry with us wherever we go.

Around twenty years ago, there were minimal sources of information. It would be either newspapers, radio, or television. Even when we spent time with them, we would consume one piece of information at a time. But now, 14 different pieces of content (Instagram feed) are presented to stimulate our senses in one second. No wonder why they have kept the name "**feed.**"

I have noticed a new trend in the content creation world - people recording their daily lives, sharing what is in their refrigerator, wardrobe, and much more. There are over a million views for these videos, which have no relation to our daily lives. But my question is, "**WHY?**"

I know it's enjoyable; I know it's relieving after a hard day. But why not consume something you need rather than random information? Eat whatever you want, but not everything you get.

CHAPTER NINETEEN

I WILL JUST BREATHE IN, I WILL NEVER BREATHE OUT

Confused? Don't you think it's odd for someone to say that they will only breathe in and never breathe out? Of course, it's a cycle. Only by breathing out can you breathe in again.

It seems obvious when it comes to breathing, but when it comes to earning money, we often think, *"I should only receive, receive, receive."* Why do we do this? The fundamental concept of money is that you get back only what you give to the world.

Think back to your life; when was the last time you paid money to someone? And what did you get in return? You might have paid for a restaurant meal, or paid a shopkeeper for a product or service that helped you.

Money is a by-product of the service or product you offer to others to improve their lives. Consider this: you paid for this book (I hope you did) because you believed that you would receive something of value in return for the money you gave me. It's always about giving before receiving.

It took me years to fully grasp this concept. I understood it, but it took personal experience to truly realize it. Every time I was paid, it was for something I had given. Compare this to your own life; what do you want to give in order to receive?

The world is filled with problems. Solve just one issue and you will be paid for it. Don't aim to solve something big at first, as it may discourage you if your expectations are too high. Start small to get a taste of how this works.

Wahei Takeda, who was considered to be the Warren Buffet of Japan, was once asked how he viewed money. Can you guess what he answered? He said, *"I see money like oxygen."* It's abundant all around us. You breathe without a second thought that you can't breathe in again (unless you're on another planet), because you know that oxygen exists unconsciously, without a doubt. You simply know that it exists. Likewise, money is abundant all around us.

Next time you think about *"how can I earn money?"* think about *"what service or product can I offer the world to improve their lives?"*

> *"The law of GIVING is very simple: If you want joy, give joy. If love is what you seek, offer love. If you crave material affluence, help others become prosperous."*

- DEEPAK CHOPRA

CHAPTER TWENTY

OTHERS LIFE IS BETTER THAN MINE

Being an Author, Coach, and Founder, I thought I didn't have an inferiority complex. After all, I have given speeches in public and on the internet, and I thought I had overcome my inferiority complex a long time ago.

One day, I traveled to another town to sell a piece of land. When I arrived, I saw big SUVs on the street and some wealthy-looking people. I started talking to some people there and suddenly had the thought, *"these people are wealthy, I wish I had a life like them."* I didn't realize I was having this thought, but I felt inferior for over an hour. I thought about all the poor decisions I've made in my life, wishing I had started earlier, made better investments, etc.

Unaware of my inferiority complex, I carried on with the conversation, pretending everything was fine. Suddenly, someone approached me and asked, *"How did you become like this?"* My mind raced, unsure of whether the question was positive or negative. I soon realized that the person's intentions were pure and he said, *"You weren't like this during school and college; I can see a huge transformation."* I didn't show any expression, but inside, I was thinking, *"What? Me? You're comparing me?"*

It was then that I realized I had done some pretty good work in the past. I may not have a million-dollar SUV, but I have made a positive impact in this world. I told the person about the books I had written and the people I had followed. It was then that I realized how I had been assuming this whole event in my mind and how different my perception was from the other person's.

I never thought I had an inferiority complex, but then I realized, *"I am not perfect either."* I believe you can relate to this topic, or else you wouldn't have read this thoroughly. I want you to be aware of this inferiority complex and be aware of it when it comes next time. The best practice is to bless the other person.

For example, if you meet someone who is more successful in the field you want to grow in, instead of comparing yourself, wish them all blessings from your heart. Acknowledge the fact that they have done their work to reach that position and simply bless them with more success.

By doing this, you are no longer operating from a mindset of lack, but from a mindset of abundance. Bless them all.

You are unique, and you know that. Everyone has their own

journey to pursue, even if we may have forgotten it many times in the past. It's not too late to acknowledge the fact that *"I am unique and I have my own journey to pursue."*

Awareness is the first key, and the second is to bless the other person. I go an extra mile when this thought arises in me; I start to repeat my favorite mantra, *"I am sorry, please forgive me, Thank you, I love you."* If you are unaware of this mantra, it is known as Ho'oponopono.

Take a deep breath, realize that you are on your own journey, and bless everyone with your heart. Blessing others doesn't require you to grow old or acquire any social standards, just do it with your heart.

CHAPTER TWENTY-ONE

DESTINY

Is our life pre-destined? If yes, then what is the use of educating ourselves? Anyhow, everything will happen on its own, right? Why should I bother to change?

I had these thoughts for a very long time running in my mind. I couldn't completely ignore the fact that destiny is a lie because I have read books and followed astrology topics for years. I have studied how planets thousands of kilometers far away affect our moods. Most religions have invested a lot of hours into researching astronomy and its effects on human beings.

You may wonder, *"So what? Do I get to choose my life or not? What if I answer you, 'YES, you do, and NO, you don't".* Confusing? Let me try to explain this as simply as possible.

"Yes, you do" Of course, you can decide how you want to shape your life through your thoughts, decisions, and actions. We have the ability to think and formulate ideas. We also have the capacity to take action to bring desired results. Through our conscious effort, we can change the course of life.

"No, You don't." It's all under the natural law. The cycle of birth and death is a natural process that cannot be changed. Any invention we make in this world bends to the laws already existing. You didn't choose your parents, that accident, or the person you fell in love with. It just happened without your conscious decision.

Natural law - It's about to rain for the next 5 hours
Conscious action - I can carry an umbrella for my commute.You can't change the fact that it is about to rain but you can carry an umbrella to travel through your conscious effort.

Let me share a story I recently heard. A religious preacher approached a house to preach the greatness of God. As he approached the house, he witnessed the beautiful garden on their lawn. The preacher, with a great smile, knocked on the door. A man opened the door with a half-smile on his face.

The preacher then said, *"Look at this beautiful garden; how magnificent is God to bless our earth with such beautiful flowers with fragrance. God's design is truly ultimate."* The preacher went on for the next 15 minutes to explain the wonders God has created on this planet earth.

The man in the house patiently waited for his turn to come. When the preacher ended his long speech, the man replied, *"Of course, God is such a powerful being. Without his blessings, none of this would have happened. But guess what? Before I visited this house, the same garden had plants and weeds in there. I took out all the weeds, cleaned the lawn, watered the plants every day, and placed beautiful rocks creating the path to this house. I didn't make the plants grow; I simply watered and cared for them, but the supreme power (Nature law) made them grow."*

The preacher smiled, and the person in the house smiled back.

Now, what did you get out of this story?

Do your own self-reflection now.

CHAPTER TWENTY-TWO

REINVENT YOURSELF

I am reinventing myself at the age of 30 and, while I may be a little scared, I am bold enough to push myself to reinvent. I have always been an explorer, and throughout my life, I have been a graphic designer, 3D modeler, photographer, NLP coach, NLP trainer, marketing manager, author, and entrepreneur. For the past three years, I have been running a company called "**The Positive Store,**" creating positive and productive products.

However, I didn't realize that each day I lived was not happy. Despite receiving recognition in the media and getting customer appreciation, I felt empty inside. The reason was that the process involved in running a business was different from what I enjoyed.

Upon deep self-reflection, I realized that I enjoyed creating the products but not the business aspect. It was hard for me to accept this fact because the company had a well-established brand with a good reputation. But the time came for me to be honest with myself.

So, I have decided to no longer continue with the business. It was hard, but I had to start again from scratch. Having this "amateur" mindset allows you to do crazy things.

"An amateur's possibilities are endless, whereas an expert's vision is fixed."

Currently, I have chosen to write, teach, and coach. I am not sure where this will take me, but I have faith that when you start to do what you love on a daily basis, the future aligns for itself.

It can be scary for many people to think about reinventing themselves. I know people who have learned a subject in college and continue to do related work for their entire lives. I am not suggesting that you quit your job, but be flexible, explore a little, and don't make safety your top priority. Remember that we will all die eventually, so there's no point in living a safe life until the end.

Most readers of this book will not be scared of the consequences of reinventing themselves, but rather worry about how others will judge them. Let me tell you, everyone has their own problems in their life. Your decision will not be of the utmost interest to others, they may gossip for a while, but then they have their own issues to deal with.

So, stop holding yourself back and reinvent yourself. Do what you believe is great work.

"I didn't see it then, but it turned out that getting fired from Apple was the best thing that could have ever happened to me. The heaviness of being successful was replaced by the lightness of being a beginner again, less sure about everything. It freed me to enter one of the most creative periods of my life."
- Steve Jobs

"Your work is going to fill a large part of your life, and the only way to be truly satisfied is to do what you believe is great work. And the only way to do great work is to love what you do. If you haven't found it yet, keep looking. Don't settle. As with all matters of the heart, you'll know when you find it. And, like any great relationship, it just gets better and better as the years roll on. So keep looking until you find it. Don't settle." - Steve Jobs

CHAPTER TWENTY-THREE

Know More About Yourself

More than knowing what your favorite celebrity eats for breakfast, what they have in their refrigerator, or what they do on their weekends, it's more important to learn about yourselves.

What do you like?
What do you dislike?
What excites you?
What makes you angry?
What skills do you have?
What passions do you have?
What is the unique trait that you possess?
Who are you?

All of these questions are simple, but they are incredibly important. These are just a few examples, and once you start to dig deep, you will enter a whole new spiritual level. In that realm, the questions change, and eventually, the questions disappear, and you just become. Now, why is it important to know yourself?

It's not just important on a spiritual level, but also in our work life. The person valued the most in society is the one who knows their strengths and weaknesses. The one who is crystal clear about what they will do and won't do. This firm certainty enters a person's life when they have a quality conversation with themselves. Not with the outer world, not with friends, not with teachers, but by conversing with oneself.

If you want to know me better, you must meet me; spend some time with me. The more time you spend with me, the better you will understand me. Likewise, if you want to know yourself, you need to spend some alone time with yourself. The most interesting person is inside you, more interesting than the movie you wanted to watch. Only if you spend time will you get to know this person better.

When you understand your needs, you will start to take actions accordingly. Later, you will only take actions that are aligned with yourself. You will not be a slave to advertising or marketing, and you will not take actions to please others.

It may sound easy to spend time with yourself, but all I can say is give it a shot and try it for yourself. Your past decisions may be haunting, but running away from them can never be a solution. You are a sum of all the past decisions you have made. The moment you accept that, you will be set free.

Action tasks:

1. No mobile,

2. No computer,
3. No digital assets
4. No books Just you! Sit idle, preferably lock your room, so no one disturbs you.
5.Take ten deep breaths to clear your mind
7. Stay silent and observe your thoughts for a few minutes; get into a meditative state.
8. Speak with yourself out loud or journal

Practice this once a week. Take accountability for your own life. No one else will do this for you.

"Be alone. Eat alone, take yourself on dates, sleep alone. In the midst of this you will learn about yourself. You will grow, you will figure out what inspires you, you will curate your own dreams, your own beliefs, your own stunning clarity, and when you do meet the person who makes your cells dance, you will be sure of it, because you are sure of yourself." - Bianca Sparacino "Knowing yourself is the beginning of all wisdom." -Aristotle

CHAPTER TWENTY-FOUR

BEING AUTHENTIC

Are you authentic? Do you do things because you truly want to or are you following a set pattern? Do you express your true interests to the world, or do you hide behind a facade in order to fit in with your peers?

How authentic are you? Not just to others, but to yourself? As Mahatma Gandhi once said, *"Happiness is when what you think, what you say, and what you do are in harmony."*

I have tried to imitate others in the past, whether it be in writing or speaking. I was inspired by legends and tried to replicate their voice, but it never gave me a sense of fulfillment. I failed multiple times because the person behind those masks was none other than myself.

When I stopped wearing masks and started expressing my true feelings, that's when I felt true freedom. It's a freedom that can only be experienced, not explained. Would you like to experience it for yourself? Try letting your soul do the work and take the egoic self a step back to see how the soul operates in life.

Authenticity means being true to yourself, not a copy or duplicate, but being in your natural state. It's rare to find people who reveal their authentic selves in their first meeting. People often wear masks and armor to hide their true selves, only revealing them to their loved ones.

Being authentic doesn't mean being vulnerable. There's a common misconception that if you're authentic, people will hurt you, and it's better to hide your true self. This may be true in some situations, but it shouldn't be a permanent state.

Why is authenticity important? If you're good at anything, it's being yourself. You don't have to imitate or compare yourself to others. When you express your authentic feelings, you align your mind, words, and actions.

There's a growing stress among young individuals whose actions don't align with their beliefs. Have you ever known someone whose actions differ from what they learn and speak?

Low self-esteem is often caused by a lack of alignment in mind, words, and actions. This can affect not only the individual, but also their relationships. Wearing a mask and pretending to be someone else is not a sustainable solution.

Eventually, the piled-up stress will break out and damage the relationship. When you're authentic, you let others know your likes and dislikes, and they can act accordingly.

Don't expect others to read your mind, the way you present yourself to the world is how you will be treated.

The biggest lesson I learned as an educator is the power of authenticity. If you've read my books or watched my videos, you'll know that I try to be as authentic as possible. When I try to mimic or act like someone else, I fail.

Life is too short to pretend to be someone else. Allow yourself to break out of your shell and be authentic.

CHAPTER TWENTY-FIVE

MESMERIZED LEARNING

Would you like to learn from someone? For example, how to sing, how to play music, how to be a good leader, or how to cook? One way to do this is by getting mesmerized. What do I mean by getting mesmerized?

Simply observe and enjoy the act performed by someone else, become an active spectator. When you become a good spectator, you start to enjoy the process. By enjoying the process, you are not consciously learning but doing it unconsciously.

It's important to note that most of our actions are unconscious. For example, when we drive a car, we make thousands of micro-actions, and it happens in a flow that you are not consciously making the choices. The unconscious mind takes care of these actions, while the conscious mind is thinking about something else.

Have you ever driven somewhere and arrived at your destination without remembering the details of how you got there? This is because the unconscious mind was taking care of the driving, while the conscious mind was elsewhere.

Similarly, a dancer doesn't consciously move their body but lets it flow with the rhythm of the music. We can make the same comparison for any other activity.

Since the majority of our decisions are made unconsciously, it's important to tap into this power when learning something new. By becoming a good spectator, you can learn faster and more effectively.

Try it out!

Action steps:

1. Find a person who does the work that you wanted to do
2. Observe them, dont take notes
3. Look at the way they work, the way they handle situations, the way they take decisions without judgement
4. Witness more of the same person or different people doing the similar work.
5. Get mesmerized.

CHAPTER TWENTY-SIX

UNDERSTANDING AND REALIZING

I thought it was the same until very recently after watching an interview online. Understanding is about knowing certain information, but realizing is about connecting that information to your life. When knowledge is not connected to one's self-understanding or if not practiced, it stays as mere understanding.

Example:

Understanding - I know that meditation is important; it helps us calm our minds. It helps us become more focused and aware of the present moment. There are different types of meditation, such as....

Realization - I have been getting anxious recently. After practicing meditation for 15 minutes, I felt calm within. So I started practicing meditation every day and guess what? I am more aware of my actions and lead a peaceful life.

You can understand any concept on the internet or through

books, but the realization is when you practice it and connect it to your life. Unfortunately, schools and colleges often focus on making students understand concepts, but fail to help them realize their importance.

Why is it important to realize?

When you don't imbibe the knowledge and execute it in your life, it has no impact on your life. You may earn a degree certificate for understanding a concept, which may help you secure a good job, but if you want to excel at it, you need to practice and realize its importance.

When you realize a concept, the same information is transferred to your subconscious, and when there is a need, you start to apply the concept without your conscious mind. It is instantaneous and does not require your conscious mind to conceptualize.

Tap into your unconscious, it is 1000 times more powerful than your conscious mind.

CHAPTER TWENTY-SEVEN

WHY SHOULD WE READ BOOKS?

(I am referring to the non-fiction books here in this chapter)

Reading books was one of the best things I have ever done in my life, and I continue to do so. At first, it was a necessity because I had certain doubts that I could not answer myself. When I started reading books, I saw that the same doubts were approached differently by different authors. These authors gave a different perspective on how to deal with them.

Reading books is not a fashion statement, a social approval act, or to prove anything to anyone. Reading books is about the curiosity you have within. Some people who do not read often associate the habit of reading with the books we read in school. During our school years, most books were forced to be read, in order to ensure good grades.

However, as adults, reading books has a different approach. Reading books as an adult is more about following the curiosity within. When you have doubts in your mind, don't think of it as if only you have this doubt, there are scholars and experts who had these doubts in their minds, and they have already crossed this. When you read their books, you get to learn their perspective.

"If I have seen further, it is by standing on the shoulders of giants"
- Issac Newton

You may disagree with the author's views, but when you read them, your perspective shifts on how you view the problem. Years of research and study have been done on that specific issue, so don't spend time trying to reinvent the wheel, read and research about the wheel that was made last year and go beyond.

Please note, some individuals boast about reading 100s of books, but when you closely look at the lives they have been living, you will know the value of the books that have impacted their lives. This is an ego-driven approach to telling everyone that they are knowledgeable, but information is of no use if it is not experienced or practiced.

"Read less but twice"
- Unknown

CHAPTER TWENTY-EIGHT

I WILL NOT PROGRESS IF I DON'T DO THIS

Seriously, no matter what ideas I get, no matter how influential people I have, no matter how many books I read, and no matter how many times I seek help from mentors, if I don't have discipline, I will go nowhere. I struggled a lot.

I had great ideas and everything I needed to achieve what I wanted, but my lack of discipline caused me to reach my destination late.

Have you faced the same? Are you aware of what you should do, but when it comes to daily actions and staying consistent, you have a problem? Well, you're not alone.

No one is our enemy but ourselves. So, what do we do now? I know that I am not disciplined, but what do I have to do?

1. Decide where you want to head.

2. Create a plan on how you're going to reach that destination.
3. Write a letter or record a video to remind yourself why it's important.
4. Put a daily action list-plan.
5. Hire a coach or a friend who can check on you at regular intervals.

It sounds simple, right? But each of these activities requires focus and dedication. Spend an entire day just to do these five activities.

Don't rush things, take it slow, one step at a time.

During this journey, don't seek perfection. You might miss a day or two, but instead of beating yourself down, rise back up. Your software (subconscious mind) is pre-installed with old patterns. When you start practicing new habits, your software gets disturbed because these are not regular patterns.

So, you might begin to tell yourself: "*Oh, this is not going to work.*" "*I was always undisciplined; I can't.*" "*Whom are you fooling? You can't be consistent.*"

It's normal to have these thoughts during the journey. But it helps to have counter-statements that oppose these low-frequency commands. When these voices arise, say statements such as:

- "I am disciplined."
- "I am not my old self anymore; I am a new version now."

- "My past was a lesson, but it doesn't define who I am." "I am in control of my life."

It's better to be prepared than unaware. Like we've discussed in previous chapters, if you have confusion, face it and deal with it. Realize your powers and what sets you apart. Set a vision for yourself and describe where you're headed and what you want to become as a person. Hire a coach to stay on track.

> *"Self-Discipline is about taking charge of your mind and directing it to act in the best interset of yourself."*
> *- Gaur Gopal Das*

CHAPTER TWENTY-NINE

NO ONE CAN SAVE GOD

I am human too, and I get irritated and angry to see news about fighting in the name of religion. The Coronavirus has made it clear that regardless of one's caste, religion, or God they worship, nature doesn't discriminate. It spread rapidly and affected people in every corner of the world, without caring about boundaries, walls, gods, or the color of a person's skin.

Despite advancements in technology and plans to establish a livelihood on Mars, fights in the name of religion continue. Some leaders take advantage of this and use it as an opportunity to maintain their leadership roles in the name of fighting for God. But the root of these emotional fights is often the manipulation of people's emotions.

I believe that God is a supreme power. There is no need to fight with one another in the name of God. The infinite intelligence is much more powerful than any of us. Fighting in the name of God is nothing but an insult to God. Claiming that one's God is superior to all others is an egoistic approach and should be treated as a mental illness.

The concept of spirituality is to overcome the ego. And I believe every religion originated to guide followers towards a spiritual path. To realize the true self and the sense of bliss that resides within is the true essence of religion. When one realizes their true self, they will not be swayed by false preachers. Let's move forward and stop playing small games.

The universe is vast and holds secrets that no one understands. Inside each of us, there lies the greatest of secrets. Let's work towards human progression and building a humanitarian world for future generations. Let's stop dividing ourselves based on color, caste, religion, and country and instead, evolve as one humanity.

"In the 17th Chapter of St Luke it is written: "the Kingdom of God is within man" - not one man nor a group of men, but in all men! In you! You, the people have the power - the power to create machines The power to create happiness! You, the people, have the power to make this life free and beautiful, to make this life a wonderful adventure Then - in the name of democracy - let us use that power - let us all unite Let us fight for a new world - a decent world that will give men a chance to work - that will give youth a future and old age a security By the promise of these things, brutes have risen to power But they lie! They do not fulfil that promise They never will! Dictators free themselves but they enslave the people!"
- Charlie Chaplin, The Great Dicator

CHAPTER THIRTY

TIME RICH VS MONEY RICH

What comes to mind when I say **"Rich"?** You may think of money, houses, fancy cars, or yachts. Most of us do this, but this is simply money rich. There is something else called **"Time Rich,"** a person who has the time to do what he or she likes.

Arguably, everyone was granted an abundance of time on this planet, but not much money. You may get rich, but that doesn't necessarily mean you will be time rich. Let's imagine you have to generate $1 million per month. What then? Would you have the time to use the money you have generated or will you be stuck in the office, where you need to safeguard this money?

I know people earning crazy rich but can't take a break if they want to. They have to ask for someone's permission weeks prior. Is it bad? No, it varies from person to person's needs. I met an entrepreneur friend who said it's his dream to have 200 employees working for him and he also added that he likes to work 8 hours a day.

Whereas I am just the opposite, I don't want many employees working for me. A maximum of three members are enough, and I wish to work 4-5 hours a day.

It's important to decide what suits you, but remember, it's not about getting money rich, but living the lifestyle you imagined. For my friend, working so many hours is what an ideal day looks like. I am not here to say which is right or wrong. Every person has a different style towards how they want to lead their life. I am just reminding you that you have a choice.

Time is the greatest asset the universe has given us all, despite gender, race, or religion. This time has been given to us for free of cost; how you make use of it differs from one person to another. And one's destiny can be predicted by the person based on how he/she uses their time.

Rather than setting goals of how rich I should be, Plan the lifestyle you would like to live.

"Don't pursue happiness. Design a lifestyle (a way of life) where the byproduct of living that lifestyle brings you joy."
- DANDAPANI

CHAPTER THIRTY-ONE

IT'S OK TO BE CONFUSED

"Confusion is very important as it let us choose something or someone and give us time to reflect on what we need."
- JESSICA COLLINS

Hey, it's normal to be confused. Every person goes through this phase of confusion in different parts of life. Suppose you are in a situation where you don't see a clear picture in front of you. It's quite normal to feel this way; Some individuals distract themselves for short-term pleasure. It could be watching random videos, using social media, or using drugs.

It may give you temporary relief, but rather than distracting yourself, accept the fact that you are confused. By accepting this, the situation may not change immediately, but you start to calm down. You get out of the anxious state and enter the mental state of being comfortable with the confusion.

Can you think clearly when you are anxious? No, right? So

let it calm down initially. Once you feel peace within you, you start to put it out in words. You could either use a journal or speak out loud. Whatever works for you. When you begin to do this, you put the problem in front of you. This means you are no more the problem; the problem is now separated from yourself.

While you sort your confusion, if at some point you feel anxiousness returns, stop planning and start to relax again. You may not think clearly when you are in an anxious state. You may derive a solution, but it may not be a long-term solution.

Some people often say you are not supposed to be confused, don't think much, just chill. But hey, just like any symptom in one's body, the mind is trying to communicate something to you here, don't avoid it. The suppression of behavior would one day outburst. It's better to confront it at an early stage. I like how Tony Robbins quotes this "**Kill the monster when it is small. Don't wait for it to grow big.**"

Great leaders, philosophers and scholars had confusions in their life. The curiosity to solve this confusion lead them into great discoveries. People who avoid these confusions work for people who accept the confusion and pursue to find an answer. If you want to be a leader, embrace the confusion and deal with it.

Step 1: Acceptance
Step 2: Confront
Step 3: Relax
Step 4: Reflect

CHAPTER THIRTY-TWO

Clean yourself

How many times do you have to clean your living space? Is there a definite number? No, right? You will have to clean the space regularly as long as you live. You may clean it on Sunday evening, but it gets cluttered again by Tuesday.

Cleaning is a regular practice that we must do to live in a peaceful space. You know where I'm going with this, right? Of course, your mind. You will have to clean it often. You may have to remove things that are no longer useful and reorganize in regular intervals. We invite a lot of junk into our minds during our waking hours.

Well, you can't clean your mind the same way you clean your living space. But guess what? We are naturally doing the cleaning process every day while we sleep. Do you remember having a fight at night and thinking you couldn't handle it anymore? The next day, you start to feel lighter about the situation after waking up.

The mind has cleared it for you. It's a natural process. All we have to do is sit back, relax, and feel good. By relaxing, I don't mean scrolling through social media. We often use social media in the name of "relaxation," but I want to remind you that you're inviting more data into your mind.

Instead, try playing soft music, lying down with your eyes closed, taking a long shower, lying in a hot bathtub with pleasant music, meditating, gazing at nature, or trying mandala coloring. Whatever suits your lifestyle, do them. But do them regularly. I know you have a busy schedule, but if you can use social media for one hour a day, you can do this as well.

Stress stops your body from healing. By relaxing your mind, you allow your mind to heal your body. When you practice this, you may feel sleepy. Don't stop yourself. Maybe your mind needs it. Allow your mind to relax, and it will do its work. Stop trying to do everything by yourself.

Your mind and body are more capable than you think. They have a chemical factory inside that has the potential to cure anything in your body. All you have to do is allow the mind to do its work.

Practice Ho'oponopono to clear all the negative blocks. Repeat these four phrases: *"I am sorry, please forgive me, thank you, I love you."*

CHAPTER THIRTY-THREE

I KEEP FORGETTING

I get an idea but then forget it. I get inspired by a speech, but then I forget. I get an aha moment from nowhere, but after three months, I wonder what I did with that?

I kept forgetting, and then I became aware that I was forgetting. This changed my perspective. I started noticing a pattern; After I get an idea, I couldn't sustain that energy because I couldn't change my routine to bring the new idea into existence because I was so comfortable with my old patterns.

I wanted to change this, but my old self didn't allow the change. So, I scheduled my day; I started to build habits that would help me execute the idea. For example, this book was started with the intention to complete within 30 days, but it surpassed 90 days due to a lack of habit.

I then used both physical planners and apps to schedule my day. Some days, I forget, but now I know where to check my ideas. It's no longer just in my mind. I have a written journal that acts as a reminder. Currently, all I have to do is go there and look at my to-do's.

Due to the overload of information we receive from multiple sources, we tend to forget our priorities and are carried away by day-to-day activities. We may feel like we've done plenty of work, but there may be little or no progress towards our purpose.

This is what has worked for me:

- A physical journal for daily self-reflection
- A digital planner, such as Asana, to plan my day
- An ad-block extension, such as Unhook, for Google Chrome to reduce distractions
- Deleting social media apps and using web browsers only when necessary
- A Pomodoro extension to help with focused work
- A letter written to myself with my end goal as a reminder if I get lost or feel down

Don't try to implement all of the above at once. It may be a shock to your system and may cause you to return to your old way of living. Also, if possible, consider quitting social media.

It can do more harm than good by feeding you with endless content and causing anxiety.

Remember, your attention is your currency.

"We have a finite amount of energy each day yet most people do not discriminate between who and what they invest

their energy in."
- DANDAPANI

CHAPTER THIRTY-FOUR

MOTIVATION DOESN'T LAST

Should you be motivated when you spend time with your child?
Should you be motivated when you drive to work?
Should you be motivated when you brush your teeth?

Well, staying motivated always is a wrong statement, which has been propagated by some people who are spreading toxic positivity just to gain your attention. To be honest, you cannot always be motivated. You have to simply be in your natural state.

You may have to be motivated when you row a boat or when you lift a heavy object, but it's not required every time.

So, when do you do your best work? While being happy or stressed? Of course, when you are happy. You are ready to climb the mountain twice for your loved ones.

Imagine the same when you are frustrated? Would you

move your finger for someone? It's natural for us to be self-obsessed when we get frustrated. The happier you are and the more happy work you do on a daily basis, the more in your natural flow you become.

That's why I advise people to choose a work that they are passionate about. 80% of our waking hours are spent on work, and if we are not happy with our work, we are unhappy 80% of our lifetime.

Death is something that no one can avoid. Death is inevitable no matter how smart, handsome, or how big your bank balance is. So why not do something that you like during this period that you are alive.

You don't have to be motivated to do a specific task, simply love the task. Love the process of working, and results will come in their own way. Arnold Schwarzenegger was once asked, *"Why is it that you're working out so hard, and you always have a smile on your face? The others are working just as hard as you do, and they look sour."*

He replied, "I am smiling because I am shooting for a goal. In front of me is the Mr. Universe title. So, every rep that I do gets me closer to accomplishing that goal. Every single set, every repetition, every weight that I lift will get me a step closer to turning this goal into reality."

While all the other bodybuilders are getting motivated to push themselves for the next workout, Arnold's end goal pulls him towards it.

Motivation is a push, inspiration is a pull. Push requires

effort, but when you have a purpose and a vision for your life, it pulls you towards your destination. Engage in more activities that allow you to be in your natural rhythm. You don't need motivation to become the best version of yourself; simply love the process.

(Disclaimer: Motivation do work, but it's like having a coffee to get pumped up. Depending on coffee the entire life to get pumped up is not healthy. So, Use it cautiously and effectively.)

CHAPTER THIRTY-FIVE

Right vs Wrong

What is right and what is wrong? Is killing a person wrong? Well, if done by the military, it's considered correct. But wait, if done by the opposite country's military, it's considered wrong.

But is killing itself wrong? Then what about meat-eaters? What about people who eat vegetables? Those are living creatures as well. What about the millions of cells that died last night while you were sleeping? There is a war happening in our body every second by the immune system guarding us.

So, what is right and what is wrong? You may disagree with my point because it is highly debatable. But this book allows me to express my views without any debate. I think right and wrong are created for moral values.

If there were nothing right and wrong, people would become barbarians with no moral values. People would eventually start to fight, kill and do more harm if there is no construct such as "Right and wrong." But I wonder how far has this gone? Although it has created stability on the planet earth, I think some people in power have taken it to the extremes.

A few decades back, color discrimination was a huge issue. People were considered untouchables. In India and some eastern regions, the division between religion and castes has created multiple chaoses. People have lost lives due to this discrimination. And Why?

Some people thought it was right! There is nothing inherently right or wrong; it's all a human construct. When the majority of people perform an act, it is often considered "**right.**" But when a smaller group of people do it, it is often labeled as "**wrong.**" Recently in Sri Lanka, when the majority of people stood against the government, it was named a "**victory of citizens.**" But a few decades ago, people who protested for similar reasons were labeled as "**terrorists.**"

At this stage, I would remind you that what we call the "**majority**" is nothing more than a group of people. Riots and discriminations continue to happen in the name of God. I wonder if God created these distinctions. If God exists in human form, I wish they would visit earth and see the consequences of these distinctions.

In conclusion, there is nothing inherently right or wrong, just different perspectives.

CHAPTER THIRTY-SIX

The Discrimination

"I am correct, and you are wrong.
My religion is the best, not yours.
My caste is superior to yours.
You come from a different street / city / state / country."

Have you encountered such people? Sometimes they might be in your family. Trust me; I am fed up with this kind of talk. But come on, great leaders have already spoken, sung, written, made movies, protested, and what not? But still, these people exist in the same world where we live.

I realized that the only person whom I can change is myself and not anyone else. Even though this book shares my perception, it cannot change you. It may influence you, though.

What we claim to be patriotism is still discrimination. Earlier, the leaders brought this thought of patriotism to unite people for the welfare of the people. But currently, the word patriotism divides people's unity in diversity.

Suppose you are a spiritual person seeking God or the supreme power; realizing that we are all one would be the first step. We are spiritual beings living in human form, experiencing this earth for a period of time. Sooner we will leave this body and transcend back to the source. Like how you hop on a taxi and leave it when you arrive at the house.

The thought of *"I am superior to you"/"I am different from you"* arises from the ego. It's funny when people say they are spiritual leaders and also say these quotes. Well, the whole point of spirituality is to dilute your ego; I wonder how they missed it.

I want to warn you, beware of such people who are influencing you. They could be in your social media, your friend's circle, or your family. A leader cannot be a preacher of hatred. History has always shown us what happens to leaders who try to divide and rule. Just telling.

"One caste, One religion, One God"
- Sree Narayana guru

CHAPTER THIRTY-SEVEN

LIVE LIKE AN ARTIST

We all have listened to music and songs, right? Have you ever wondered what mental state the artists were in when they wrote or composed that art form? They are also human, but what makes them different from the usual person? I am a huge fan of Kamal Hassan; he is an actor, dancer, singer, producer, etc.

When he was asked how he could do all these works, whereas ordinary people struggle just to perform one role, he answered, *"I am surprised with how this all works. I am just playing, and I am getting rewarded for that. It's as if the world is asking the child to play more for which the child will be rewarded."*

He didn't consider the activities as work but rather play. When we play with our friends, we don't think to climb the stairs or jump over the wall, but when the same instruction is given as work, we tend to see the same activity as a burden.

"Forget the dancer, the center of the ego; become the dance. That is meditation."
- Rajneesh

When an artist is involved in the creation, they become it. The singer becomes the song, the painter becomes the painting, and the dancer becomes the dance. They are it, and it is expressed.

A person who experiences the art becomes the art itself. That's why people cry when they listen to music. Something in them connects with the art; it resonates within their deepest self. The vibration from which the artist expressed can be met when you are ready to leave your current vibration and revibrate in the vibration of the artist.

"I dream my painting, and then I paint my dream."
- Van Gogh

When you lose yourself and surrender, you experience the art as it is. Vijay Sethupathi, one of the refined living actors in this generation, once said that he doesn't learn from anyone or take notes. He simply admires the art, and when he admires it, he says that it imbibes within him.

When you listen to a song, switch off the logical mind; rather, experience the song as it is. Experience it; let it do its magic without your conscious effort.

We all are artists. You have an art form in you that only you can feel. Embrace it, love it, and express it.

"We don't read and write poetry because it's cute. We read and write poetry because we are members of the human race. And the human race is filled with passion. Medicine, law, and engineering these are all noble pursuits and necessary to sustain lives, but poetry, beauty, romance, love, these are what we stay alive for."
- A Scene from the movie Dead Poet Society, narrated by Robbin Williams

CHAPTER THIRTY-EIGHT

SIEZE THE DAY - CARPE DIEM

You and I are all going to die one day. The truth is obvious, isn't it? We are going to turn into dust; there is going to be an expiration date for each one of us. No one knows when it's going to happen, but everyone knows that it will definitely happen.

No wise men, rich people, or the most intelligent have ever escaped death. We all share the same destination in the end. So, what do we do until then? Are we going to pass through this life safely? If yes, then for what? Anyways, your death is inevitable.

When this naked truth hits you in the face, you stop worrying about petty things you tell yourself *"Oh, not now, I'm not ready yet, I don't want to look stupid, I don't want to stand out from the crowd, etc."*

None of these matters when you accept the universal truth that your body has an expiration date. You do what you are supposed to do; if you don't know what it is, then search for it. You will find what you search for, not what you wish to search for. This day, the present moment you are living now is a gift. What are you doing with it?

There is no definite answer to what is to be done. Everyone is different in how we want to seize the day. But the question is, are you doing what you promised you would do? Or at least in the pursuit of finding what you should do?

It's up to you to answer this question. Don't let doubts stop you. Doubts are nothing but your creative mind used in the wrong way. The possibilities of failure are predetermined by this mind and are called doubts. But I invite you to use this creative imagination power to think about what could possibly go right? How would it be then?

Take a deep breath and seize the day.

"Yesterday is history, tomorrow is a mystery, and today is a gift... that's why they call it the present."
- Master Oogway

CHAPTER THIRTY-NINE

STOP TRYING AND START BEING

"Don't try to attract the bees; you be the flower."

The moment you try to, you are not. Rather be that. If you want to write, don't think about writing, just write. If you want to dance, don't think about dancing, just dance. Who is to say what is right or wrong when your soul within smiles when you dance? Whose permission are you waiting for to experience the joy within?

You may seek appreciation, but no appreciation matters to the soul within until it expresses its true self. Don't block your own expression; let the expression express itself. You become the awareness that experiences the expression itself.

Poetic, isn't it? I just wrote it in a flow. I never thought if it was the regular way of writing or not. Not sure if it will be accepted by standard publication rules, which decide what is good or wrong. But I'm just expressing what is within me. Who's permission do I need to be myself?

You too. Whose permission are you waiting for to be "**you**"? Don't let perfectionism fool you; the other word for perfectionism is insecurity. You can only grow during the process. A child walks at its own pace; the child doesn't aim to be a perfect walker; the child falls a thousand times, yet enjoys the process of standing up, leaning forward, placing the foot right, balancing the hip, adjusting the shoulders, moving the neck, balancing the weight using the hand. It's a process.

The child never knows all the above, but the curiosity in the child helps the child to do these activities. Where did we lose this? When did we lose our curiosity?

The curious person needs no guidance; the search itself takes the person to distant lands. If you have an idea, rather than researching about it for endless hours, take action on it *(Unless it actually requires research work).*

Analysis paralysis:
When you have too much data, you become incapable of choosing the path. Sometimes it's better to know less; information overload leads to anxiety. Take some time to breathe and let go of the thought that "you are not enough."

Affirm to yourself:*"I am enough. I have all the resources within me. All that I have to do is to express it through my work. The universal intelligence is communicating through me."*

CHAPTER FORTY

THE INNER TALK

If everything is to be simplified, if you need to find out the crux of our problems in life, it is our inner talk. We speak with ourselves every single day, "*Should I read this or listen to music? Should I eat now or later? Should I switch on the AC or not? Maybe I should get a haircut; maybe I will start following my passion. If I take a long holiday, maybe I will become more productive...*" It goes on.

We are not speaking it out loud, but we have this talk within us every day. Have you ever thought of waking up early and working out but failed to do so? The same mind was energized and excited to go to the gym the previous day, but the next morning, you would say to yourself, "*Not today; let's go tomorrow. My bed is so comfortable! According to the health experts, I have to get 8 hours of sleep, and I slept only for 6 hours, so not today!*"

When we stop listening to our promises, we call it procrastination. So, what do super achievers do to get rid of this procrastination? They simply deny this little voice; instead, they project their vision in front of them. When they remind themselves about the destination, the little voice loses its power over persuasion.

"When you have a vision, a very clear vision of what you want to look like, then you cannot wait to do the next set, or the next exercise, or the next rep, because you know that each rep you're doing, each set your doing, each weight you lift, you get closer to turning this vision into reality."
- Arnold Schwarzenegger

Arnold Schwarzenegger used to have a big bodybuilding picture in his bedroom, so the moment he woke up, he gets reminded of his end destination. How often do you remind yourself where you are headed in life? Most of us are distracted by multiple things in our daily lives. Like a monkey, the little voice seeks instant gratification, like having a cup of tea or ice cream or watching that useless video on the internet.

I personally knew this concept of inner talk for more than five years, yet I found it hard to get my life straight. That's when I was introduced to "**Autosuggestion**" by Joseph Murphy; this can also be called a personalized affirmation.

Write down the problem you are facing in your life and later convert it into a positive affirmation as if the divine intelligence has already executed the thing you wanted the most.

Example: I have financial troubles and wish to earn more.

Repeat this affirmation:
"The divine intelligence is flowing through me. It has blessed

me with abundance and is currently blessing me as well. This divine flow is bringing all good fortunes into my life. I am experiencing luxury and comfort. I am in love with my life."

Repeat this thrice during the day and once before going to bed. So, why does this work?

Remember that we have an inner dialogue with ourselves? Well, you can't argue with it every time. You won't have all the time to convince it; this inner dialogue jumps from one area of life to another. If you could simply sit in a relaxed posture and repeat these affirmations internally, these suggestions get ingrained into your subconscious.

Once the subconscious accepts this idea, it does everything possible to bring this new idea into reality. Affirmations you find on the internet might not solve your problem, so personalize your own affirmation.

Step 1: Write down 1 problem in your life
Step 2: Convert it into a positive statement that affirms that you already possess or are that.

Example:

Problem: I am confused with life
Affirmation: I am exactly where I am supposed to be in my life. The answers are coming into my life on a daily basis.

Problem: I lack self-confidence and I am shy.
Affirmation: I am confident. I am strong in my ideologies. The universe communicates directly through me.
Problem: I am poor and wish to have more money.

Affirmation: I am wealthy. I get wealthy ideas. People around me support me to grow wealthy. I have X amount of money in my bank account currently. I am great at managing my money.

The logical mind may intervene and try to convince you by saying *"it's not true"*. It is quite obvious that it does, but remember that you are the master of your mind and not the other way around. Just like how a horse obeys its master's commands, ensure that you are the master and direct your mind towards your desired destination.

"You must see it. You must believe it. And then you must never stop working to make it happen."
- Arnold Schwarzenegger

CHAPTER FORTY-ONE

HAS IT OCCURRED YET?

The so-called problem that you claim to have - has it occurred yet, or has it just existed in your mind for years now? 95% of the people who are reading this don't have crucial problems in their lives that could potentially kill them in a few days. Some countries struggle to get clean water and are dying because of malnutrition.

Yet, most of us have been given all the basic necessities such as food, shelter, and family. To those people who claim that they are living a bad life, let me tell you this: you are fighting for growth, not survival. There is a difference between growth and survival.

I'm not asking you to sit back and relax or not to worry. But the problems that you claim to have in life are solvable. They require clarity and perseverance to solve.

Most of us have problems in our heads, but not in our present lives. The so-called problem hasn't occurred yet in reality, but you've built it in your mind. If you can see it in your mind, you can hold it in your hand. This means that you will create your life according to the mental image you hold in your mind. Reality is kinder than your thoughts; focus on what good exists already in your life and build on it.

But suppose you do have a severe problem that is non-solvable. In that case, your stress makes sense. Otherwise, use your imagination power for something useful. Growth is necessary, but suffering is not.

CHAPTER FORTY-TWO

MESSAGE TO THE CREATIVE PEOPLE

Are you a creative person? Who thinks beyond the social construct? Who questions the matrix? Who finds beauty in unknown places? Who expresses their emotions in your unique way?

Well, here is a shout-out for you. You are much needed in this world. More than any other time in history, you are in demand. The world needs more creative individuals who question and make people wonder beyond.

But the sad fact is that most creative individuals are stuck in the algorithm. With thousands of experts' help, the distraction algorithm has created platforms such as Instagram, Facebook, Twitter, etc.. These platforms may sound pleasing and promising, but the ugly truth is that it demands your awareness.

Have you ever wondered how something could be provided for free yet become a global brand? Well, your attention is their income. The more time you spend on their platforms, the more they can earn. Advertisers love this new age of marketing because they can now pinpoint their customers based on their age, gender, demographics, and interests.

So, what's the problem? How does it bother you?

For creative individuals to express their art to the world, they need solitude. When they spend time alone in their minds, a sense of boredom arises, which later turns into creative thinking. Social media doesn't allow you to get bored.

A true artist needs to keep their mind clean. The more it is clean, the more it can express; when an artist starts to consume random data, the art gets polluted. It becomes the sum of everything consumed by the artist.

Contained energy: An author takes months or years to craft a single book. The same applies to all creative individuals. Some take days, months and even years, depending on the art form, but the algorithm demands consistency daily.

Well, you can't demand your mind to stay creative every day; there are times when artists feel like not working for days, and that's ok. But the algorithm doesn't appreciate it. Due to this, we start to create content now and then. The pressure to create content daily just to be on this hamster wheel is not worth it. Remember that your art has its own rhythm.

Isn't social media required to express your skills? Social media indeed helps you showcase your work to the world.

But we don't just share the content on social media but become approval seekers. When you share a piece of content out to the world that you think is valid, it may not get the views or likes you expect.

This may be due to the algorithm and nothing to do with your art. But most people tend to connect this with their art and lose faith in it. We are artists; we are in the business of making art, not seeking approval. The internet is the most powerful tool invented by humans; use it wisely.

CHAPTER FORTY-THREE

NO YOU ARE NOT SUPERIOR

No, you are not superior, and neither am I. If lightning strikes us both, no matter what god we worship, we will eventually die.

No matter where you and I graduated, we will die if we fall from a rooftop. Nature doesn't play favorites; it is we, the humans, who do. Anyone you witness on the street is no better or worse than you. We are all made of the same blood, vessels, and nervous systems.

No medicine works for one caste of people and not for others. This delusion of separation causes disharmony in people's lives. We live in a century far removed from discrimination. Even when the majority follows this discrimination, we the people can change the minority into the majority.

In the spiritual world, there is no separation. You are a bag of energy, and so am I. When we are viewed at a microscopic level, we are this bag of energy moving around, touching another bag of energy.

Of course, people do become experts or good at something through hours of training, but there is no bias regarding caste, religion, or even demographics.

The delusion of a superior mindset might make you feel alone in the world. On the other hand, feeling inferior makes you not express your true self. So, learn the art of balancing it. Learn to respect others and also yourself.

CHAPTER FORTY-FOUR

FIND A BEST FRIEND FOR LIFE

Wouldn't it be amazing to have a best friend for life? Someone who sits beside you, cracks jokes, takes care of you, supports you during tough times, teases you, watches movies with you, and cries with you? If you stop seeing your spouse as someone above you and instead view them as your friend, I'm sure they would want to feel the same way.

A friend is someone with whom we don't hesitate to share our secrets, because we trust they won't judge us. *(They may tease us, but they do it to lighten the mood.)* While other chapters in this book may be serious, what's the point of living if we can't laugh?

"There are some people who could hear you speak a thousand words and still not understand you. And there are others who will understand without you even speaking a word."
- Yasmin Mogahed

How true is this quote? Have you ever met someone who doesn't understand you, even after talking for hours? That's the kind of person you should avoid. Unfortunately, some people spend their entire lives with someone like this. In India, it's considered normal to adjust and live with your partner once you're married. The amount of mental pressure a person goes through during this period of life is unimaginable.

If you're in a similar situation, please seek help from a relationship counselor. Adjusting isn't a way of life; rejoicing and accepting your partner is. This happens because of society's so-called *"rules."*

Stop worrying about what others will say. Take charge of your life and take responsibility for your decisions instead of blaming others. If you're single and looking for a relationship, search for a good friend. It could be a girl or a guy. If you find someone with whom you can share your weird ideas, laugh with, plan your life with, and share your ideas with, go for it. You have nothing to lose, and you may gain a lifelong partner.

If that person is your true friend and doesn't feel the same way, they won't hate you; they'll make fun of the incident and make you feel better. What if the other person also feels the same way but is waiting for you to make a move? Or what if they had no idea about your feelings but are open to the possibility? The options are endless. There's no harm in trying, but make sure you feel that your friend could be your ideal life partner before making a move. The world is vast with many places to explore, so take your friend with you to experience new adventures. Happiness multiplies when shared.

"Friendship is the purest love"
- Osho

CHAPTER FORTY-FIVE

WHERE THE HECK ARE WE?

If I locked you in a room, wouldn't you wonder where I am? We live on this small planet, not too far from the sun to freeze or too close to burn; we are in the perfect position for water to form, allowing us to comfortably live our lives. But where are we?

For millions of kilometers, there are no other beings we have spotted to call neighbors. Scientists claim that we live in a galaxy with clusters of stars, and they also say there are multiple galaxies similar to this. But who put us here? Or did we evolve as Darwin claims? Or were we space travelers who crash-landed on Earth?

But why? Are we some kind of algae growing in a Petri dish in a science lab? Scientists are still making progress in understanding where we are, and some so-called human beings are fighting over whose God is superior.

But wait for a second; where are we? Are we living in a simulation? Are we inside a supercomputer like a game?

Where all the characters think they are operating on their own, but there is a gamer who controls the character? There are high chances that we could be in a simulation; why? Well, in a computer, the basic language is 0 and 1. There is a set of algorithms and patterns that keep the computer running.

The universe we live in can be derived from that by claiming that everything we experience comprises of 3 elements: Electron, proton, and neutron. This acts as a central axis that exists in the rock and our brain. Could this be the computing language of the simulation?

Recent discoveries go beyond these three elements and claim that everything is a wave and not a particle. We are advancing in our understanding of this reality, and still, we are *"work in progress."*

We experience only through our senses. How can we say what we see is real if we are aware that our sense perceptions limit us from experiencing this world?

Our brain recognizes, formulates, and derives a conclusion only based on the inputs given to our brain. But what if there are multiple variable inputs that we are not aware of which exist?

Our human experience of eyes could only perceive colors such as red, orange, yellow blue, green, indigo, and violet, which can be derived by combining the base three colors Red, yellow, and blue. At the same time, pigeons perceive an extra color beyond violet, which is ultraviolet.

Does that mean pigeons perceive realities that are not visible to us? This expands the level of possibilities that could potentially exist. I wonder why the Hindu philosophers call the reality that we perceive as Maya. Could they have understood this concept long before the scientific theories?

To better understand this concept, imagine yourself playing a Grand Theft Auto game in a VR headset. You have the freedom to jump off buildings, ride motorcycles, interact with others, and do virtually anything, within the limitations set by the programmer. If you were to play the game long enough, you may forget that reality exists beyond the VR headset and believe what is displayed on the headset to be real. However, this doesn't mean that your physical body doesn't exist.

The connection between dreams and simulations:
The movie Inception has clearly portrayed the concept of dreams. When we are in a dream, we perceive it to be reality. We experience pain and physical touch, and there is a sense of time and space within the dream. We believe everything to be real, even though our mind is creating these experiences. We forget that we were asleep in our bedroom just a few hours ago.

When we wake up, we realize that it was all just a dream, but our body still reacts to the illusions created by our brain. The irony is that when we are dreaming, there is no starting point, and we don't know how we entered that plane of existence. Similarly, when we are born into this human form, we know that we exist, but where we were before entering this human body remains a mystery.

Could it be possible that we are in our own dream right now?

CHAPTER FORTY-SIX

IT'S MY RESPONSIBILITY

It's because of my family,
It's because of the country I live in,
It's because of my husband/wife,
It's because of my teachers.

NO! Your life is your responsibility. All the external people might have influenced your life, but the decision-maker was always you. You may say that you didn't have a choice, but the sad and ugly truth is that even then, you had a choice.

Imagine a map with dots. Each dot you have taken in the past lead you here reading this book. Even this present moment is a book from where you travel again. I am a huge fan of the movie **"Cloud Atlas".**

In that movie, you will see how small actions taken in the period of 1936 affected the lives of people living at 2321. They quote, *"Our lives are not our own. We are bound to others past and present, and by each crime and every kindness we birth our future."*

Life is not random or chaos. The tiny causes created in this lifestream create multiple effects, which in turn cause significant changes.

Imagine if graham bell, the founder of the telephone, was forced to become a cop due to family pressure. You might not experience the benefits of an evolved version of mobile phones. If that were the case, mobile apps would not have been in the time frame in which we live.

Arguably, suppose some other genius invents the same telephone machine in a different period than the Graham bell. In that case, it creates multiple repression, due to which we may not experience the same world as we live in the present date.

A small act creates a major shift in the world. If 1 person could change the entire history of the world, so can you. Your 1 decision shifts your life completely, and guess what? You always had and will have this choice.

The more I fool myself that it's not me, my parents, my society, and my teachers, the farther I go away from the truth and experience suffering. Instead, accept that *"My life is my responsibility"* and set yourself free from the illusionary jail you have built for yourself.

CHAPTER FORTY-SEVEN

RISK EARLY

Seriously, What are you waiting for?

Do you want to sound professional? Are you scared of getting embarrassed? Will your little heart get hurt if someone ridicules you? Seriously? What is stopping you?

Like the Nike logo says, **"Just do it".** I don't know what age you are, but I am telling you that you can do it now; stop overanalyzing every act of yours and jump into action. You will learn during the path rather than sitting idle.

If you have an idea that you believe in, spend time with it, learn from it, discuss it with others, research about it, work on it and be persistent until you are satisfied with the output.

A bad plan is better than a no plan; when you start to take action on the idea, it starts to improve, and what appeared to be a vague idea starts to re-organize and start to take new shapes. After plenty of iteration, it becomes a beautiful shape, and then people around you ask, *"How did you do that?"*, and all you have it says is that *"I started"*.

Every day the time is ticking, and you are 1 day closer to your death. It may be hurting, but the fact is that we all are going to die someday, and the irony is that no one knows when. All that I would say to you is don't die with your skills, ideas and dream. Share it with the world.

Do you know when a ship is safe? When it is in the harbor. But it was not built to stay in the harbor till it gets rust. It is meant to go roaring across the waves, challenging nature and pursuing its destination. Is it not risky? Of course it is risky, but it was built to encounter the challenges.

Don't live safely till your death bed, in the end, you will regret the actions you wish you had taken. Cut the chains which is holding you back, push them back to the past where it belongs and walk forward to the future with that great smile of yours.

"The biggest risk is not taking any risk... In a world that is changing really quickly, the only strategy that is guaranteed to fail is not taking risks."
- Mark Zuckerberg

CHAPTER FORTY-EIGHT

FEELING GOOD IS THE SECRET

"Insanity is doing the same things and expecting for a different result"
- Albert Einstein

If you do what you have always done, you will get what you have always got; this is not magic, It's basic common sense. Why do we do it, though? Why do we sabotage ourselves consistently if we know that it will make our life even more miserable? We are programmed in such a way.

We are programmed to be cautious and act out of fear. Most of the advertisement invokes a sense of **"fear of missing out"**. As we already discussed, we are safe now. You have a roof on top of your head, a meal to eat, and you know where you sleep tonight. It's time to feel good now.

The problem is not the problem, but the feeling that we have associated with the problem is the problem. Remember the time when you encountered a problem with a positive attitude? You simply crushed it. What made it possible was your attitude.

The game is filled with challenges, but it becomes fun with a positive attitude. See your life also like a game. With the attitude of feeling good, you see your end destination; clearly, your mind becomes creative in giving you ideas on how to reach the destination faster. Your mind becomes your friend rather than your enemy. All you have to do is to feel good.

"Certain people think they will feel good if a certain things happen. The trick is: you have to feel good for no reason." - RICHARD BANDLER

You don't have to wait till the finish line to feel good; start to enjoy the journey as you go through the process. Most of us fail to realize the simple fact that feeling good makes us feel good.

We all need happiness; we are literally programmed to be happy. Some think if they get a beautiful wife, they will be happy, some think if they get a million dollars, they will be happy; some think if I could help 1000 children, I will be happy, It's all true. We are, in one way or another other seeking happiness. The shift that I am asking you to make here is to feel good during this journey.

Still not convinced?

"You become what you think about"
- Napoleon hill

"All that we are is the result of our thought"

- Buddha

"You create your own universe as you go along."
- Winston Churchill

For a very long period in my life, I thought that I was creating my universe only while I visualized for 5 minutes during the morning. I failed to realize that I have been crafting my life throughout the day using my feeling. You can't expect to eat one carrot every morning but to drink alcohol all day long yet still expect to be healthy, would you? Well, I did, for a very long time period, unconsciously. Now am consciously shifting my mood to feel good for no reason.

Start to make this shift in mind to feel good consciously. The secret to doing this is very simple **"Smile".**

Now smile!

CHAPTER FORTY-NINE

WHAT STORY DO YOU TELL YOURSELF?

Do you know that we are directing our life movie? If our life was showcased in a theater, we would be the director of this film. How?

Let me share with you this story of 3 monks.

After three years of deep meditation in the jungle, three monks were returning to their village. As they approached a lake, they found that the usual boatman was not present.

The two disciples began to complain, "*What a tragedy, we can't cross the lake. How will we get to the village?*" But the master responded with gratitude, "*Thank you God for giving me another day to stay in the forest. How kind of you.*"

The disciples were surprised by the master's reaction. As they searched for shelter, they came across an old, rundown hut. The disciples complained again, *"How can God be so cruel? Why is he doing this to us?"* But the master expressed gratitude, *"Thank you for giving us such a wonderful place to stay."*

The disciples could not understand their master's perspective. However, as they settled into the hut, a storm began and the roof blew away.

The 2 disciples started cursing God now, *"How cruel can you become? What did we do to you? We have meditated for 3 years in search of you, and is this how you treat us?"*

The master now started dancing in the rain shouting, *"Oh god, Thank you for the rain. It was so long that I took a bath; you knew this and showered me with rain at the right time. How kind are you? How kind are you?"*

The disciples got angry now and asked the master, *"How can you lie to yourself like this? Don't you see that this is unfair? How can you praise God for putting us in this situation?"*

The master paused for a moment and replied, *"Hmmm, I don't know if god really is testing me or not, But at least my way of thinking makes me grateful what about yours?"*

End of the story.

How kind is God? How kind is God?
You know the world is not bad, nor is life; it simply depends on the meaning we give to it.

Have you encountered such personalities who find fault in everything that happens to them? On the contrary, are people who find joy in regular life simply happy the way life is?

Now imagine you take these two personalities to the most beautiful place in this world. The complainer will find fault even if the best is delivered. At the same time, the other person jumps in joy.

What is happening here?

We are our own story tellers in our life. The events occurring in our life have no meaning but the meaning we tell. If you lose your job, it means different for different kinds of people. Some view it as the best time in their life to explore the possibilities; some go into deep trenches, worrying about how they will repay the debt, and some view it as an opportunity to raise their standards by applying for a senior position job.

The same event has different stories in the minds of different people. Now, what decides this? It's your mindset. Let's practice saying better stories to ourselves starting today. List down 10 things that are fantabulously great in your life right now! DO IT!

I would suggest you watch this movie called **"Life is beautiful - (1997)"** and I dare you not to shed tears at the end of the movie. It's such a beautiful movie that I would suggest it to anyone who says life is unfair or cruel.

Try it for yourself, and let me know!

CHAPTER FIFTY

None Was True

All that you read in the previous chapters are not true. They are my perspective of the world. Live your life and learn it yourself.

Conclusion

Hope you enjoyed reading my book. Please do leave your honest review on amazon. I encourage you to check out my other books which are available at Amazon.

1. 25 Small habits
2. 55 Questions to ask yourself
3. Comfortable slaves
4. Know thyself
5. 50 Things to realize before it's too late
6. Aligned work

9 798890 023575

Printed by Libri Plureos GmbH in Hamburg, Germany